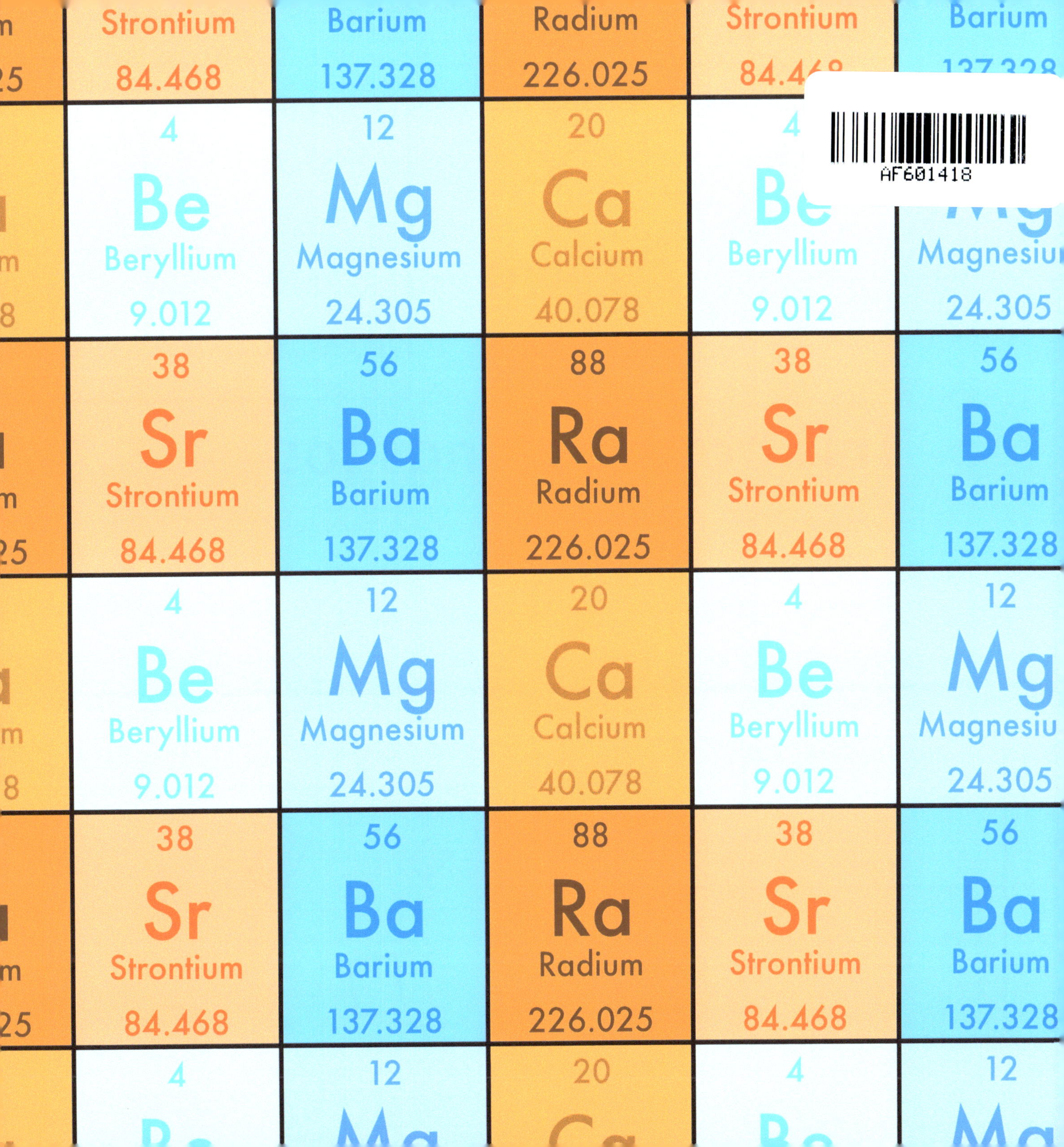
Strontium
84.468
Barium
137.328
Radium
226.025
AF601418
4
Be
Beryllium
9.012
12
Mg
Magnesium
24.305
20
Ca
Calcium
40.078
Beryllium
9.012
24.305
38
Sr
Strontium
84.468
56
Ba
Barium
137.328
88
Ra
Radium
226.025
38
Sr
Strontium
84.468
56
Ba
Barium
137.328
4
Be
Beryllium
9.012
12
Mg
Magnesium
24.305
20
Ca
Calcium
40.078
4
Be
Beryllium
9.012
12
Mg
24.305
38
Sr
Strontium
84.468
56
Ba
Barium
137.328
88
Ra
Radium
226.025
38
Sr
Strontium
84.468
56
Ba
Barium
137.328
4
12
20
4
12

This book belongs to:

4
Be
Beryllium
9.012
12
Mg
Magnesium
24.305
20
Ca
Calcium
40.078
38
Sr
Strontium
84.468
56
Ba
Barium
137.328
88
Ra
Radium
226.025

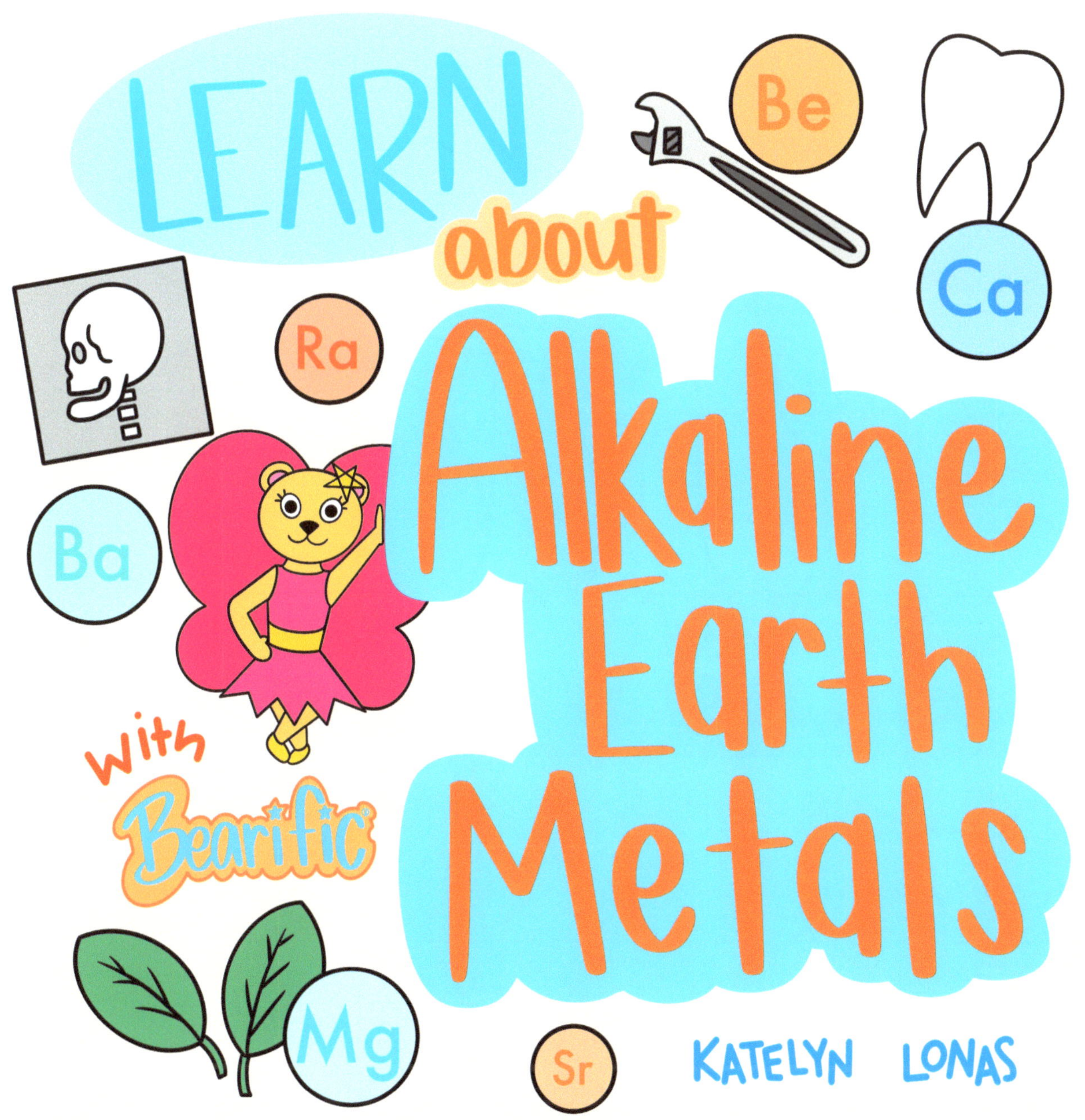

KATELYN LONAS

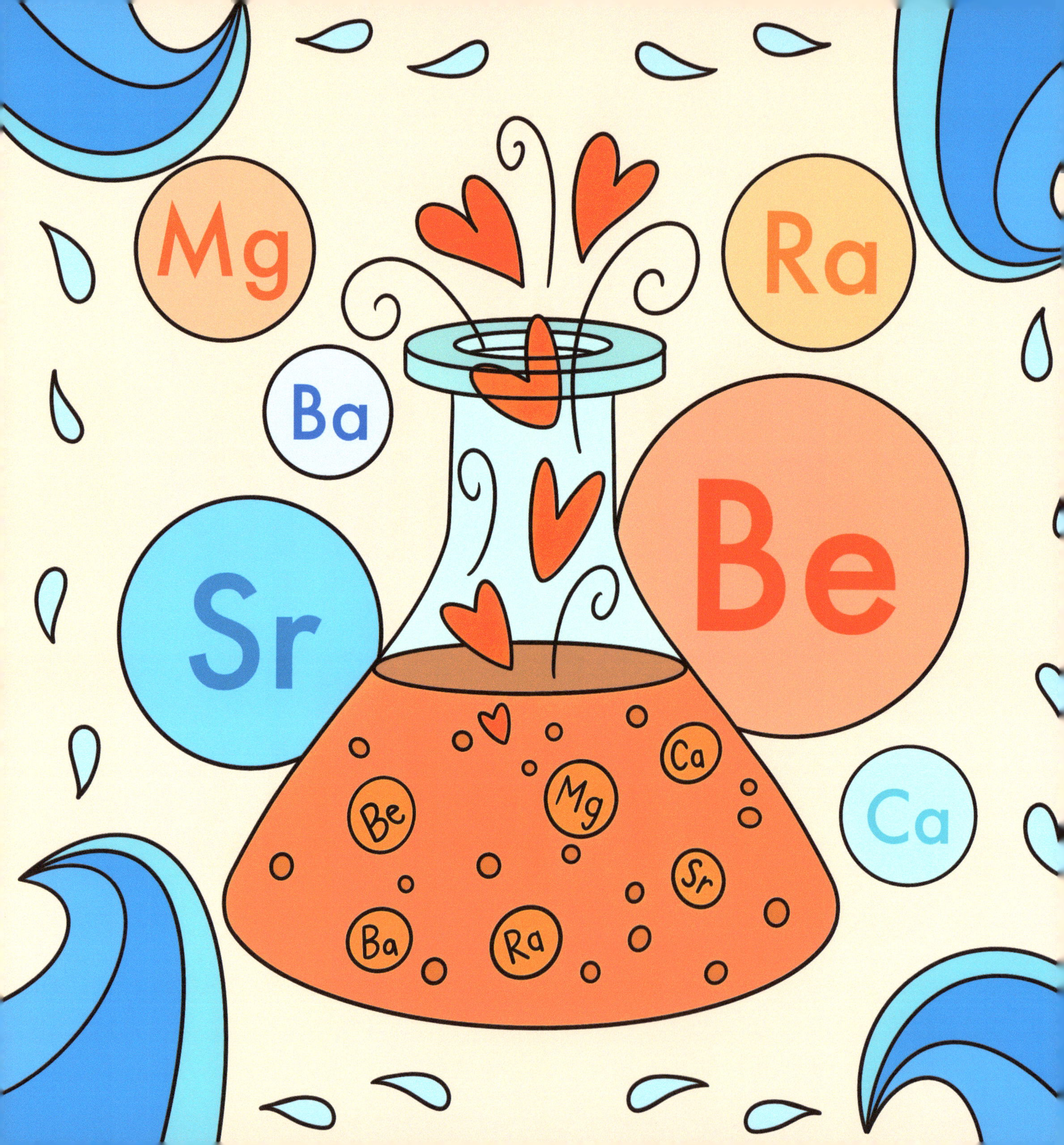
Mg
Ra
Ba
Be
Sr
Ca
Ca
Be
Mg
Sr
Ba
Ra

About Alkaline Earth Metals

Alkaline earth metals consist of six chemical elements. They are shiny, silvery-white, and are relatively soft metals. Alkaline earth metals can be fairly reactive under standard temperature and pressure.

The Periodic Table of Elements

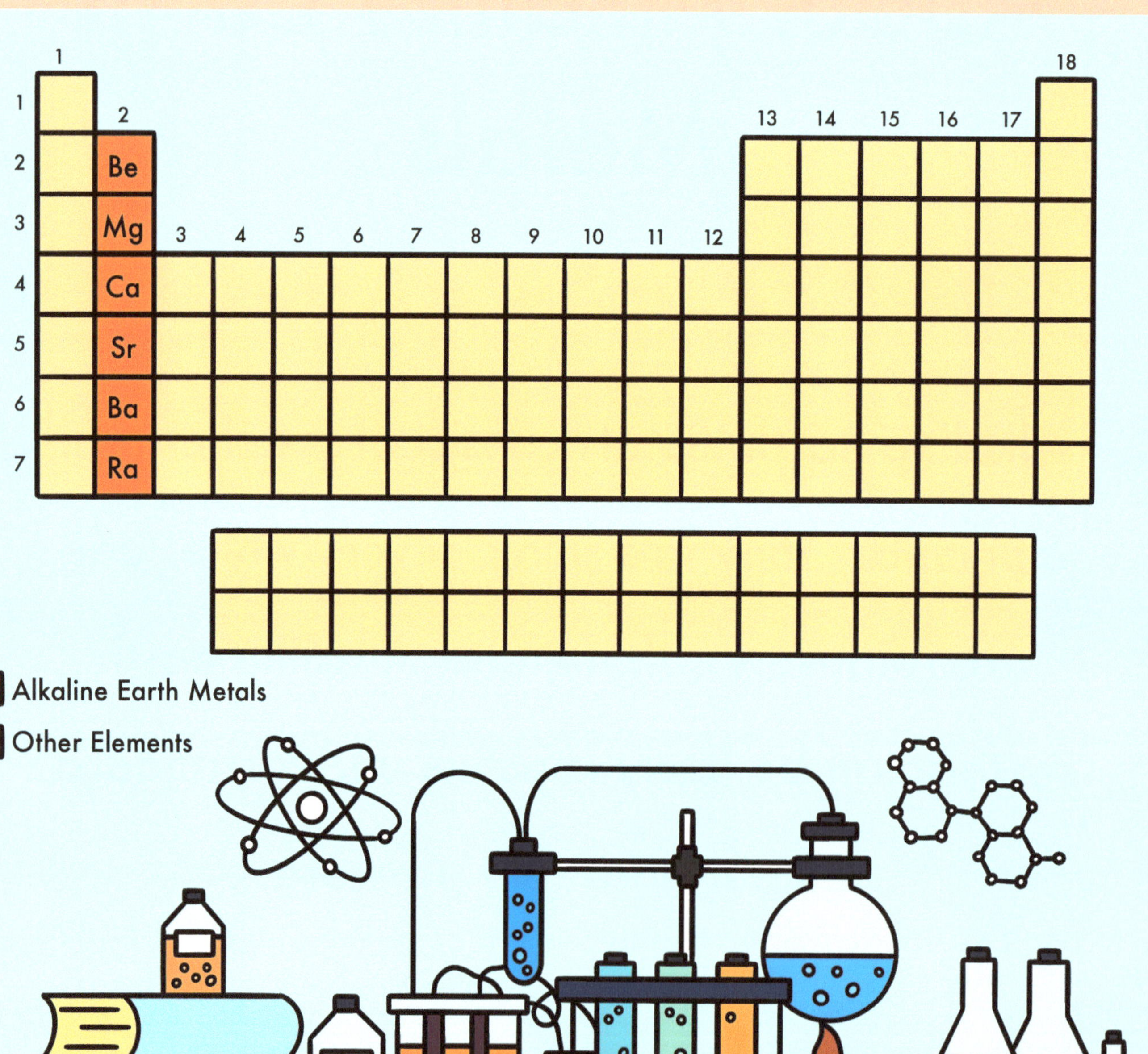

The Periodic Table

Alkaline earth metals are a group of chemical elements from the s-block of the periodic table. Alkaline earth metals make up Group 2 of the periodic table and they have 2 valence electrons.

Alkaline Earth Metals History

Alkaline earth metals have been studied since 1798. It was named after their oxides, the alkaline earths, whose old-fashioned names were beryllia, magnesia, lime, strontia, and baryta.

Beryllium

Beryllium

Beryllium is a light, silver-gray, soft metal that is strong, but brittle.

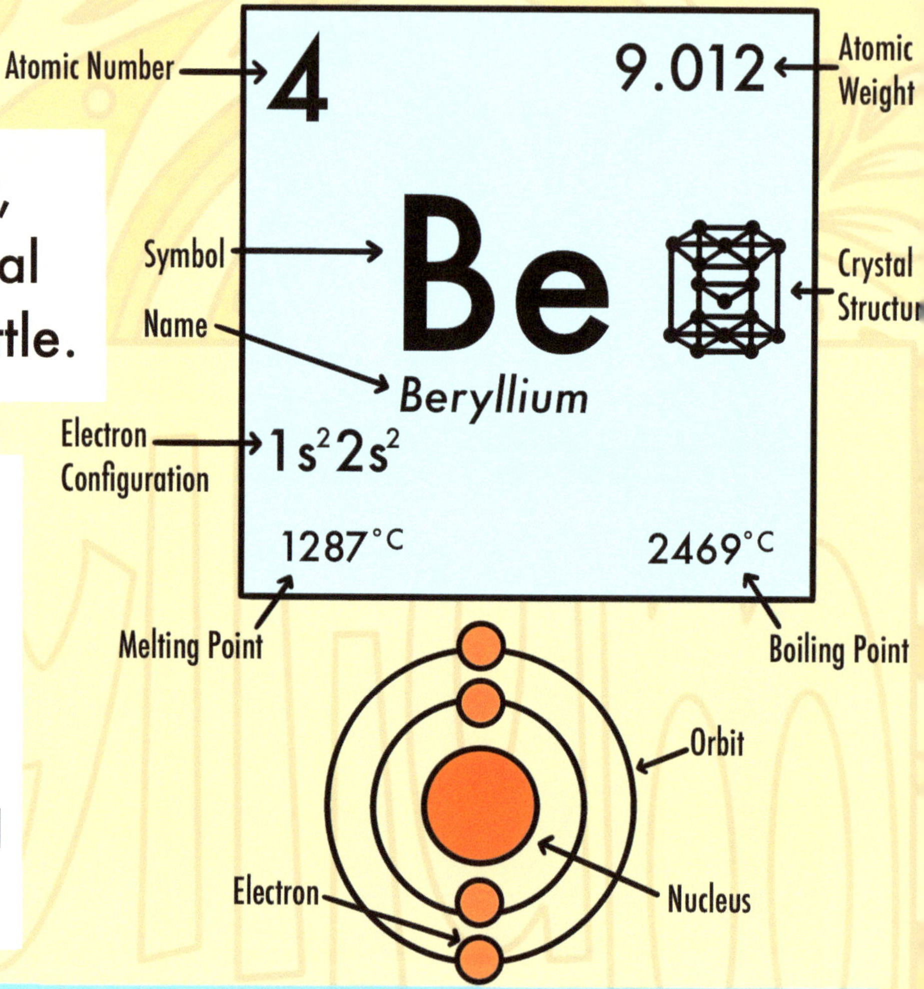

Beryllium toxicity can cause difficulty breathing, weakness, fatigue, loss of appetite, weight loss, joint pain, coughs, and fevers.

Atomic Number → 4

Atomic Weight → 9.012

Symbol → Be

Crystal Structure

Name → *Beryllium*

Electron Configuration → $1s^2 2s^2$

Melting Point → 1287°C

Boiling Point → 2469°C

Orbit

Nucleus

Electron

It can be used in gears and cogs particularly in the aviation industry. Beryllium is used to transmit precise electrical signals to delicate surgical instruments and monitoring devices used in the newest, non-invasive surgical techniques.

Beryllium was discovered in 1798 by the French chemist Louis Nicolas Vauquelin.

Beryllium occurs naturally in the Earth's crust. It can be found in the air, soil, water, and in volcanic rocks.

What contains beryllium?

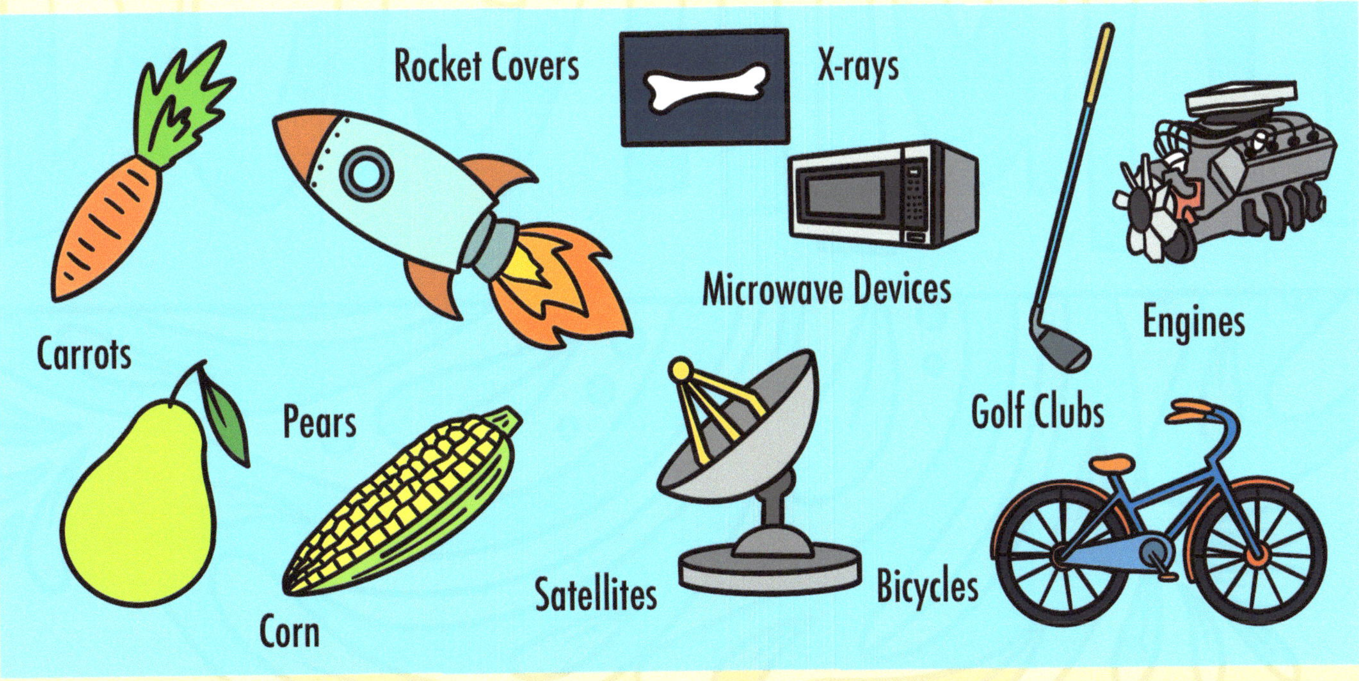

Carrots

Rocket Covers

X-rays

Microwave Devices

Golf Clubs

Engines

Pears

Corn

Satellites

Bicycles

Magnesium

Magnesium

Magnesium

Magnesium is a silvery-white metal that ignites easily in air.

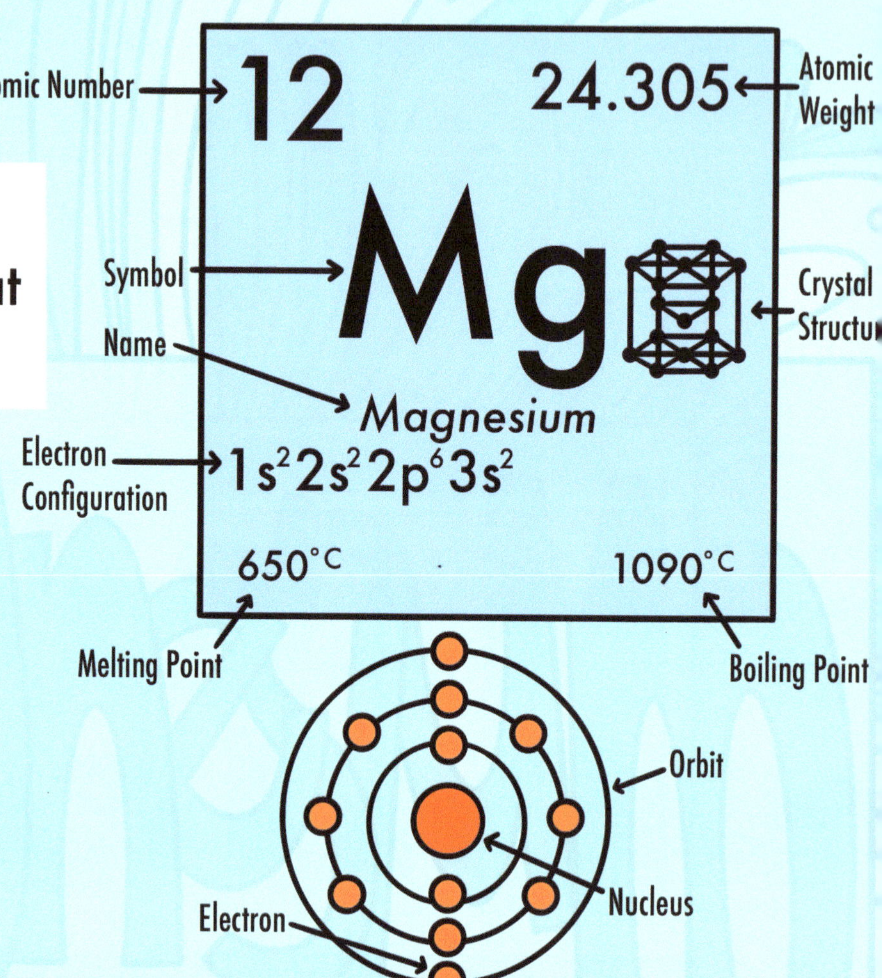

Magnesium toxicity can cause hypotension, nausea, vomiting, depression, difficulty breathing, extreme hypotension, and irregular heartbeat.

It can be used in car seats, luggage, laptops, cameras and power tools. Magnesium is also added to molten iron and steel to remove sulfur. Magnesium is important to health and is most commonly used for constipation.

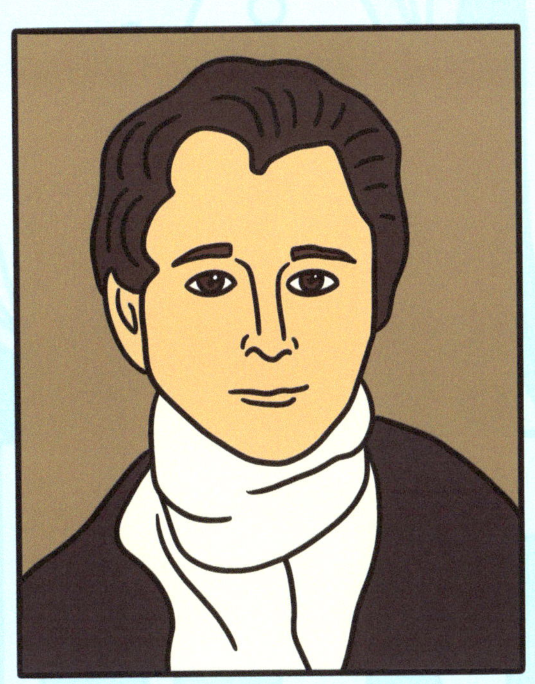

Magnesium was discovered in 1808 by the British chemist Sir Humphry Davy.

Magnesium does not occur uncombined in nature and is found in large deposits in minerals such as magnesite and dolomite.

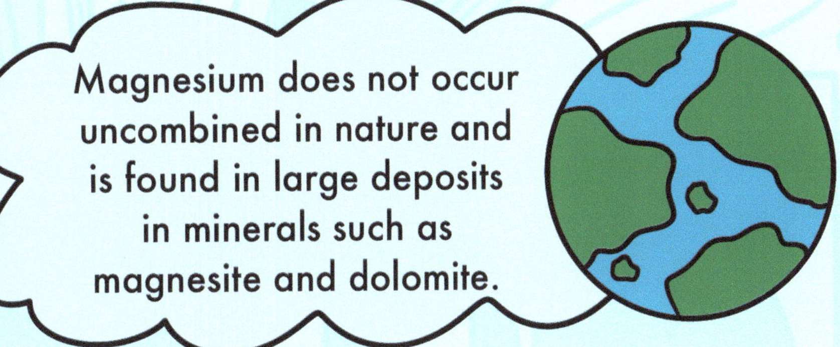

What contains magnesium?

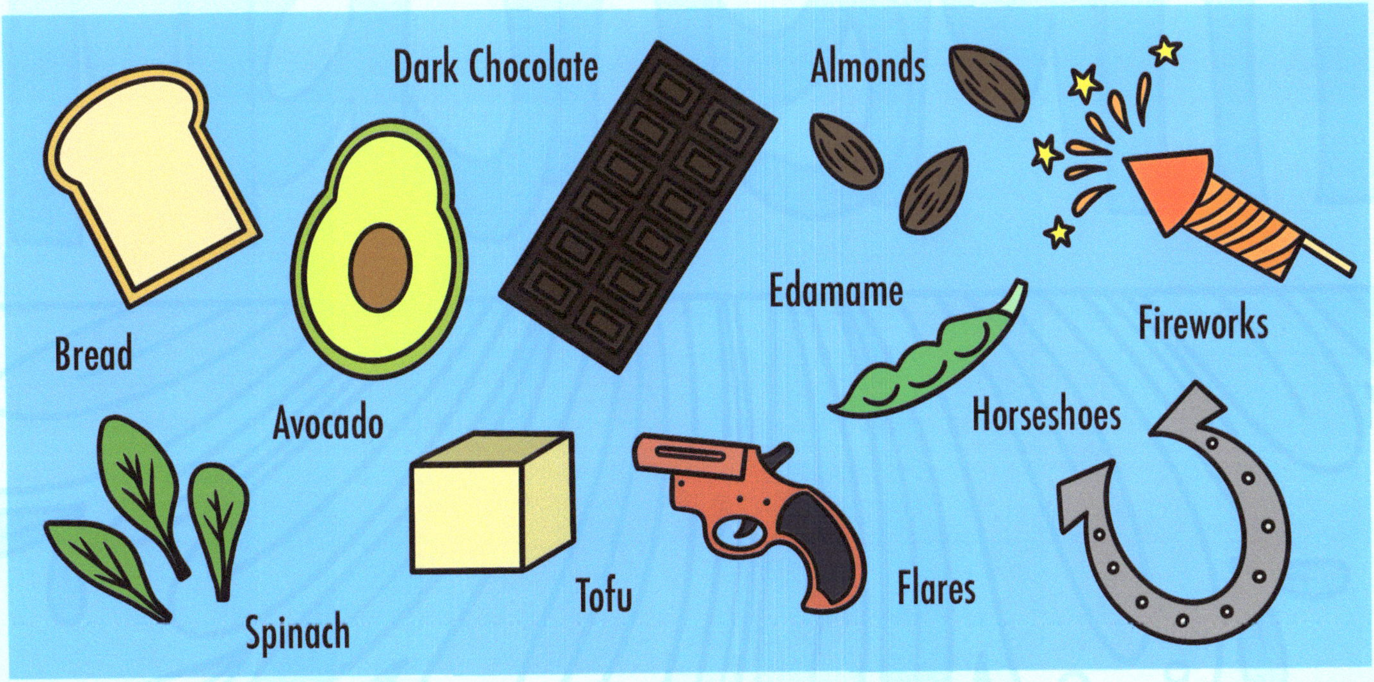

Dark Chocolate
Almonds
Bread
Avocado
Edamame
Fireworks
Horseshoes
Spinach
Tofu
Flares

Calcium

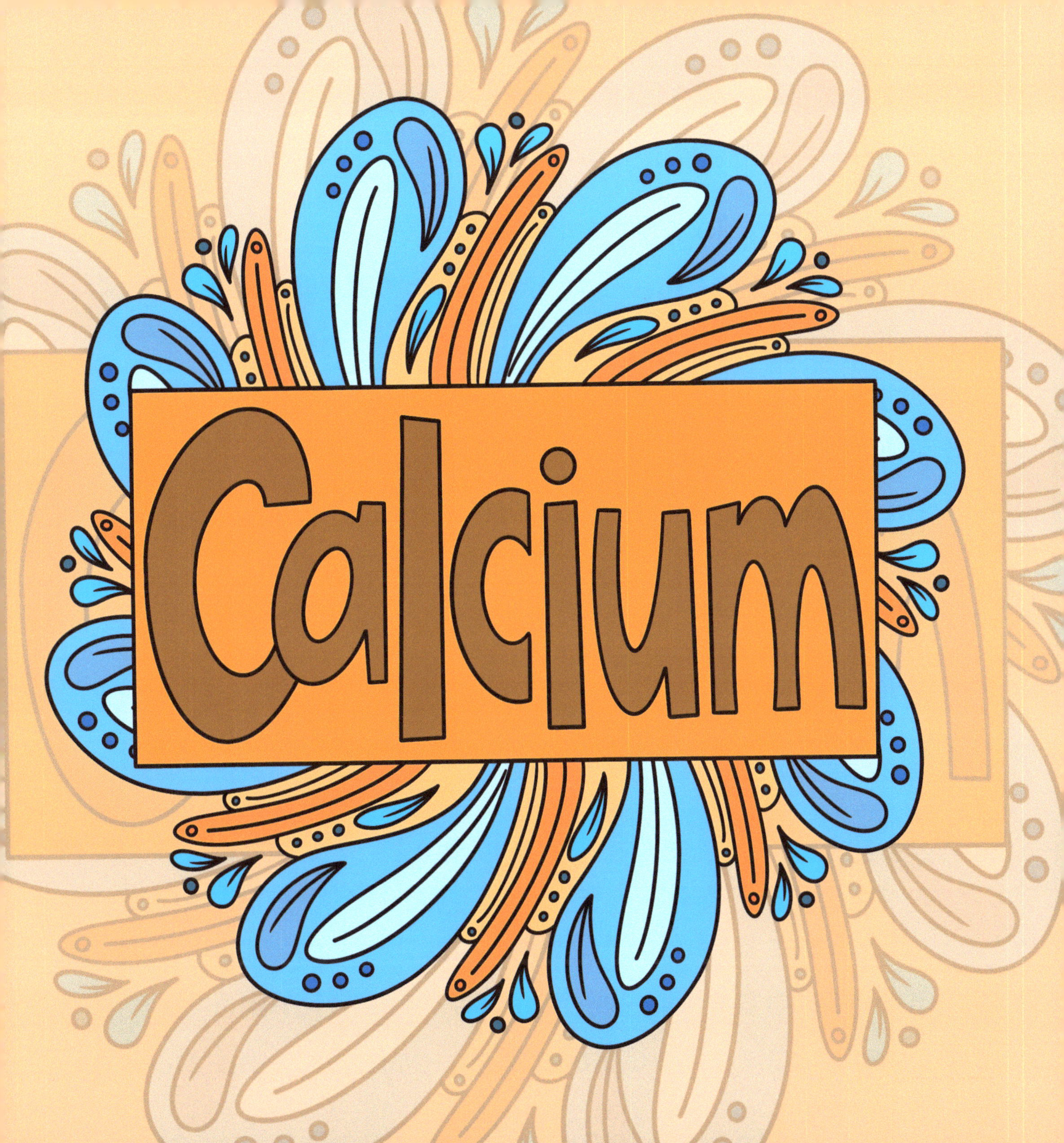
Calcium

Calcium

Calcium is a silvery-white, soft metal that tarnishes rapidly in air

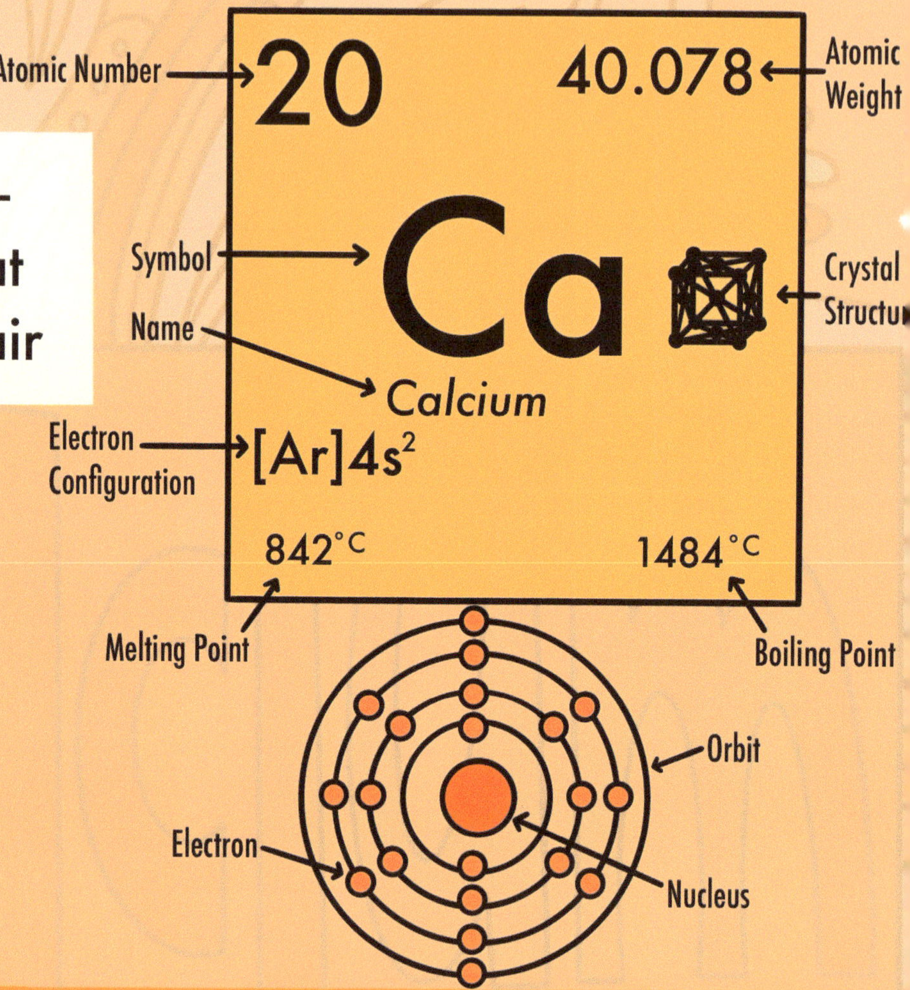

Calcium toxicity can weaken your bones, create kidney stones, and interfere with how your heart and brain work.

It can be used used to make cement and mortar. Calcium is also used in the glass industry. Calcium is used in treatments and preventions of muscle cramps, osteoporosis, softening of the bones, high blood pressure, cancer, and strokes.

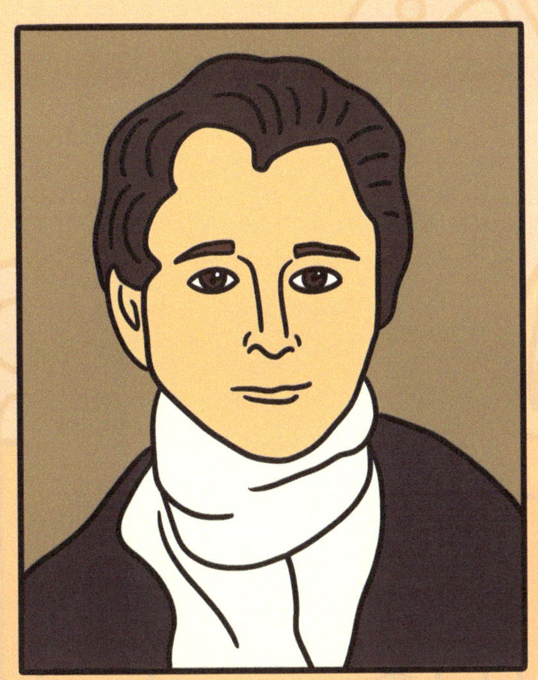

Calcium was discovered in 1808 by the British chemist Sir Humphry Davy.

Calcium does not occur uncombined in nature and is found in the Earth's crust and oceans.

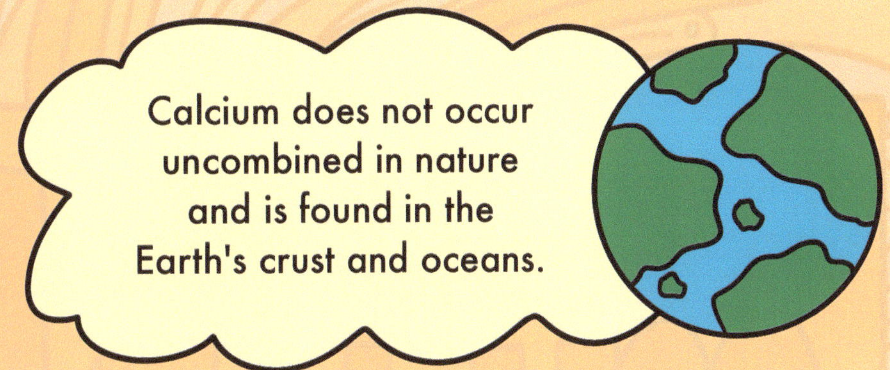

What contains calcium?

Salmon
Yogurt
YOGURT
Sardines
Ceramics
Kale
Cheese
Paint
Milk
Eggs
Broccoli

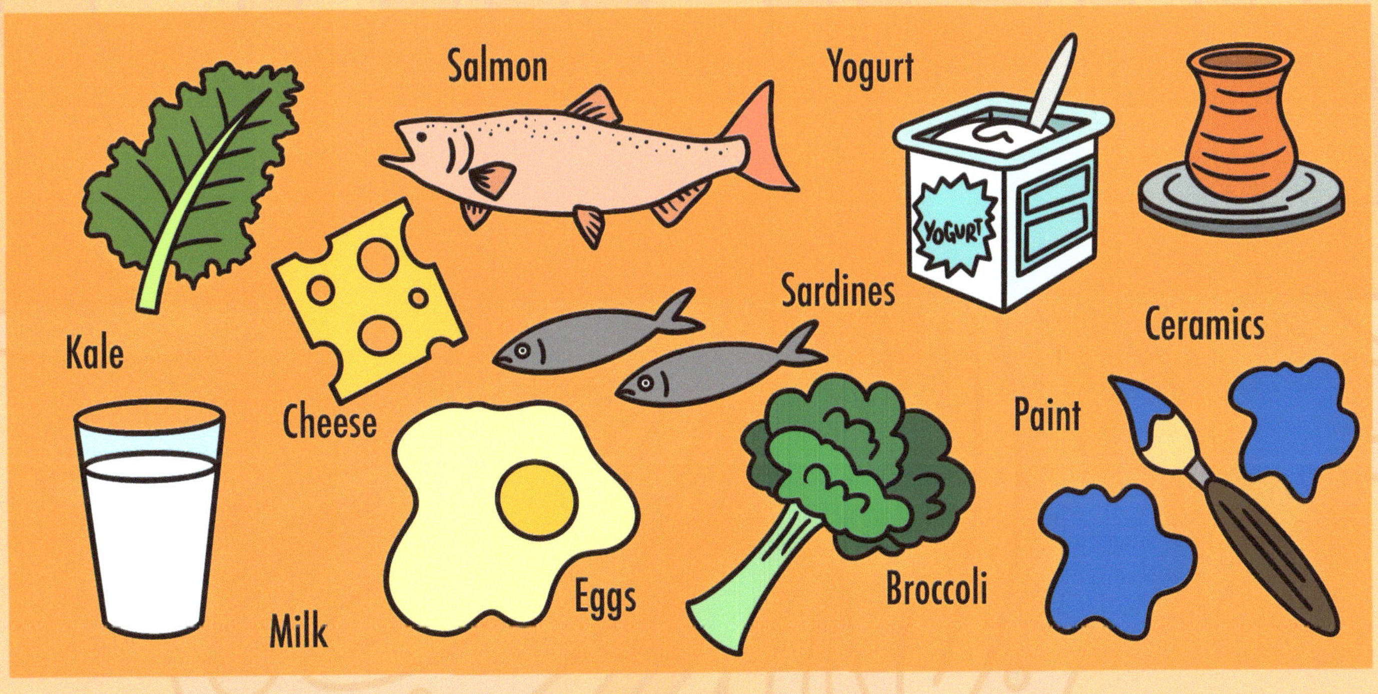

Strontium

Strontium

Strontium

Strontium is a silver-yellow metal and is known as a bone-seeking element.

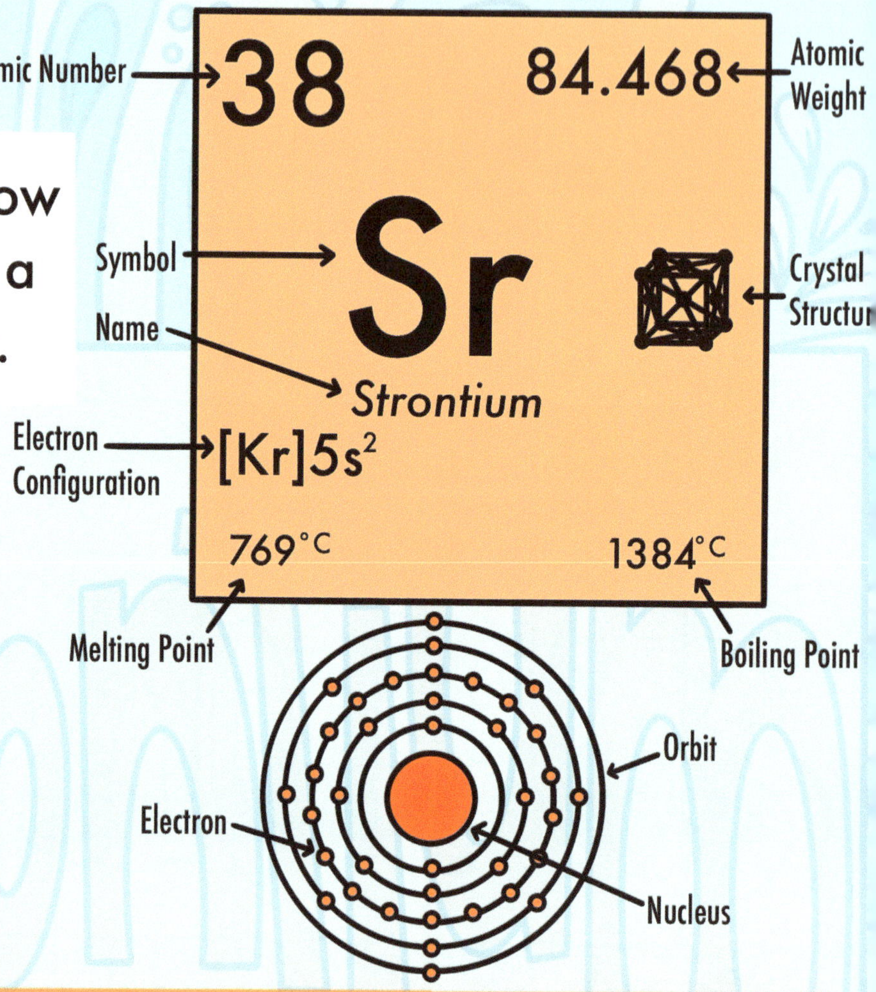

Strontium toxicity can cause stomach pain, diarrhea, headache, drowsiness, high fevers, muscle pain, heart attacks, blood clots, and clogged arteries.

It can be used in producing ferrite magnets and refining zinc. Strontium is also used in glow in the-dark paints and plastics. Strontium can help reduce bone pain, increase bone mineral density, and reduce the risk of some fractures.

Strontium was discovered in 1808 by the British chemist Sir Humphry Davy.

Strontium occurs naturally in the Earth's crust and is found mainly in the minerals celestite and strontianite.

What contains strontium?

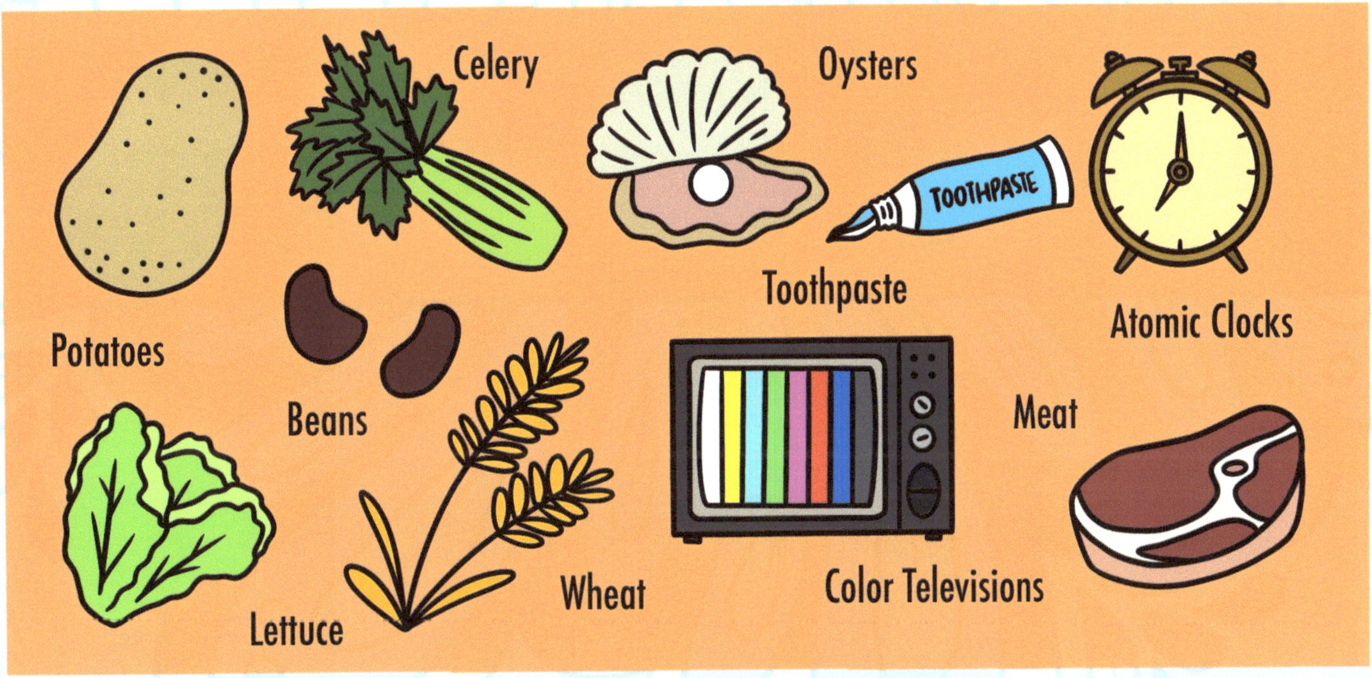

Potatoes

Celery

Oysters

TOOTHPASTE

Toothpaste

Atomic Clocks

Beans

Lettuce

Wheat

Color Televisions

Meat

Barium

Barium

Barium

Barium is a soft, silver-white metal and is a solid at room temperature.

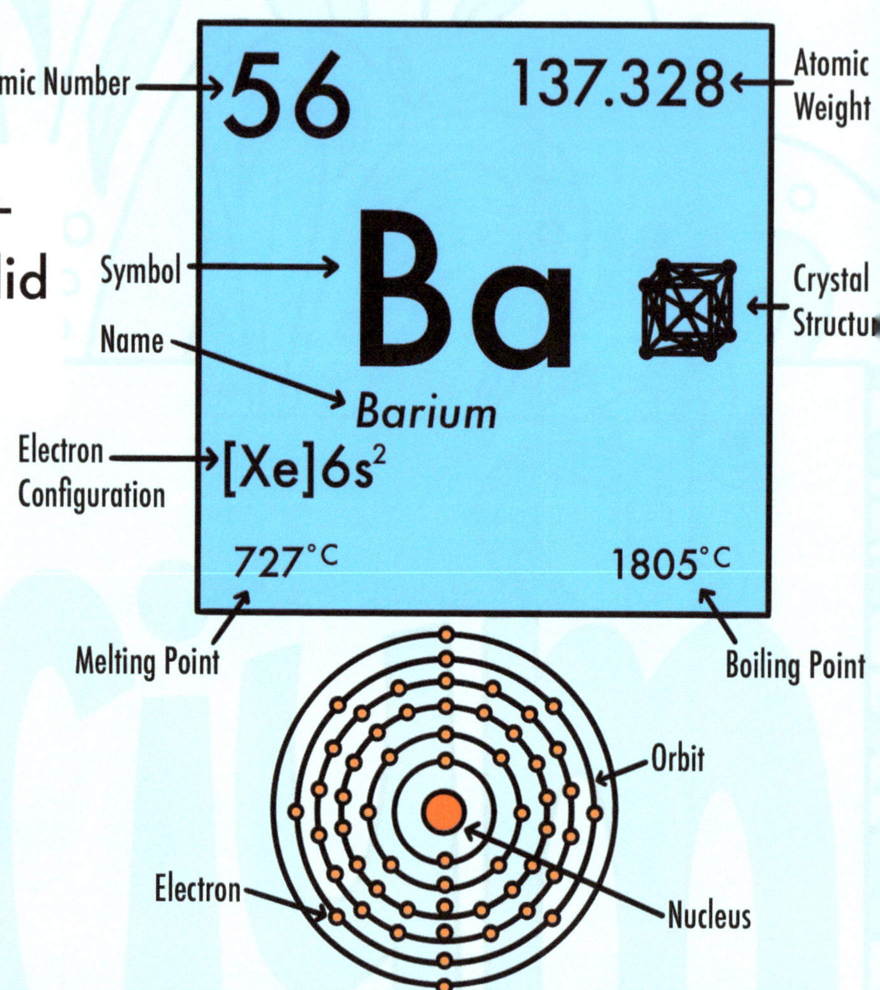

Barium toxicity can cause vomiting, diarrhea, abdominal pain, hypokalemia, hypertension, cardiac arrhythmia, and skeletal muscle paralysis.

It can be used for spark-plug electrodes. It can also used in vacuum tubes as a drying and oxygen-removing agent. Barium is used to help diagnose and find certain disorders of the esophagus, stomach, and bowels.

Barium was discovered in 1808 by the British chemist Sir Humphry Davy.

Barium is found naturally only in combination with other elements like igneous rocks, sandstone, shale, and coal.

What contains barium?

Fish

Fabrics

Onions

Glassmaking

Poison

Brazil Nuts

Paint Making

Seaweed

Cereal

Oil

Radium

Radium

Radium

Radium is a silvery-white color that can turn black when exposed to the air.

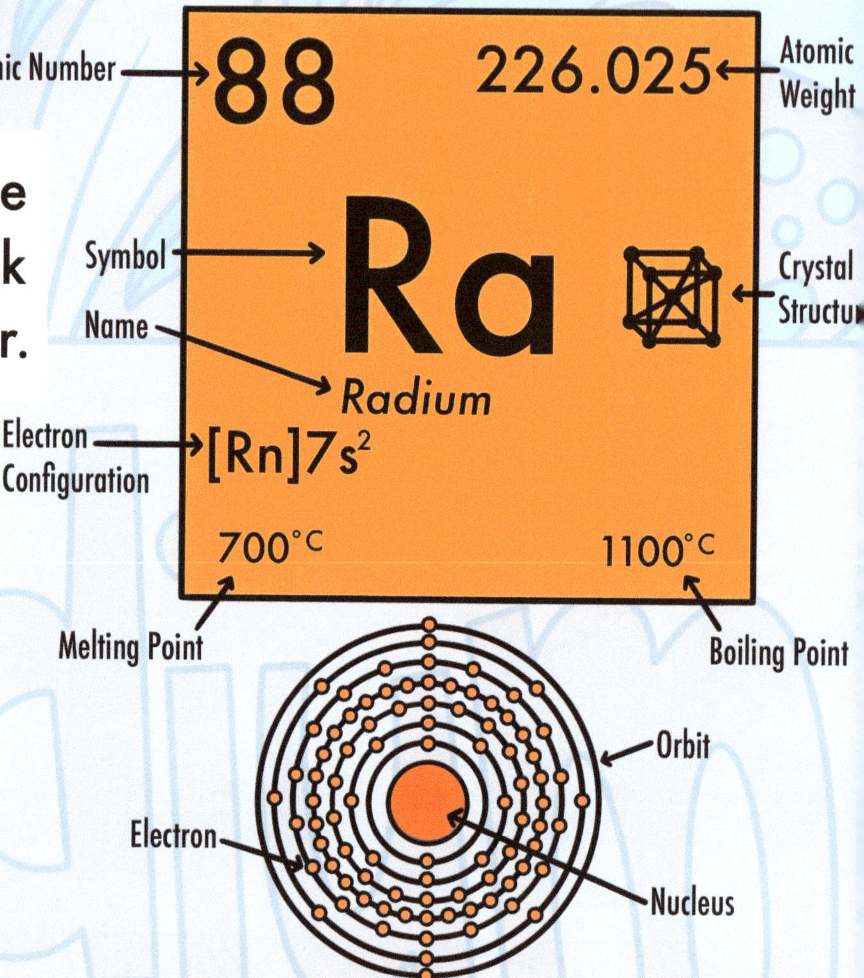

Radium toxicity can cause nausea, vomiting, diarrhea, headache, fevers, dizziness, disorientation, hair loss, and stools from internal bleeding.

It can be used in medicine to produce radon gas, used for cancer treatment. Radium has been used in numerous industrial and consumer applications. Many use to believe adding radium to products somehow made it better.

Marie Curie

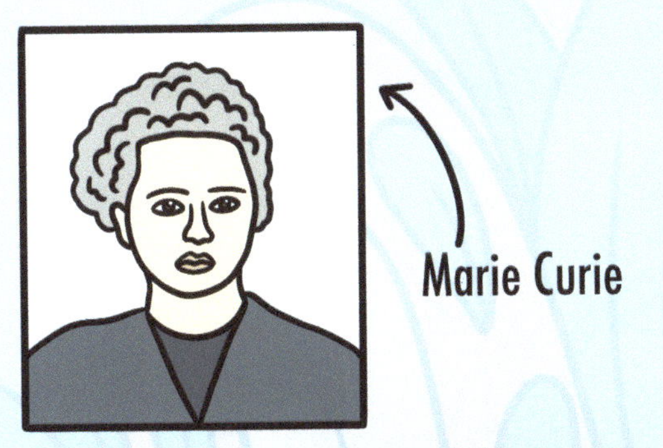

Radium was discovered in 1898 by the French chemists Pierre Curie and Marie Curie.

Pierre Curie

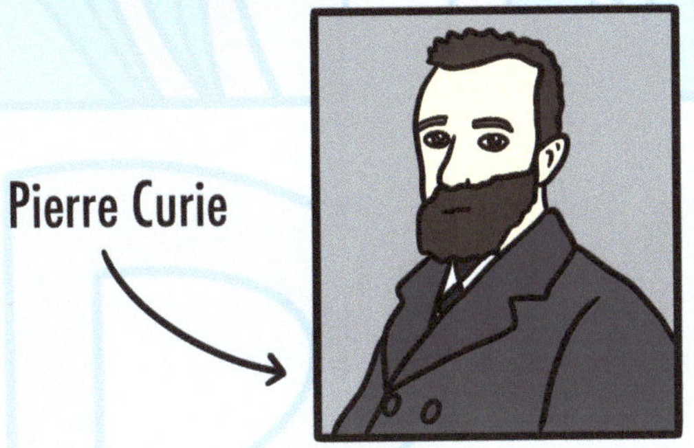

Radium occurs in nature, and can be found in rocks and soil within the Earth's crust.

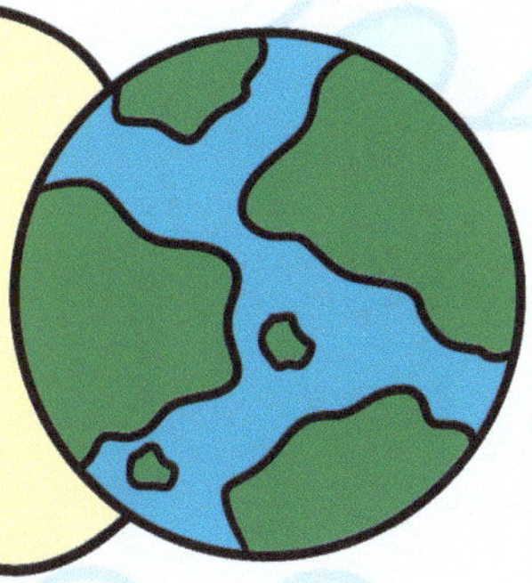

What contains radium?

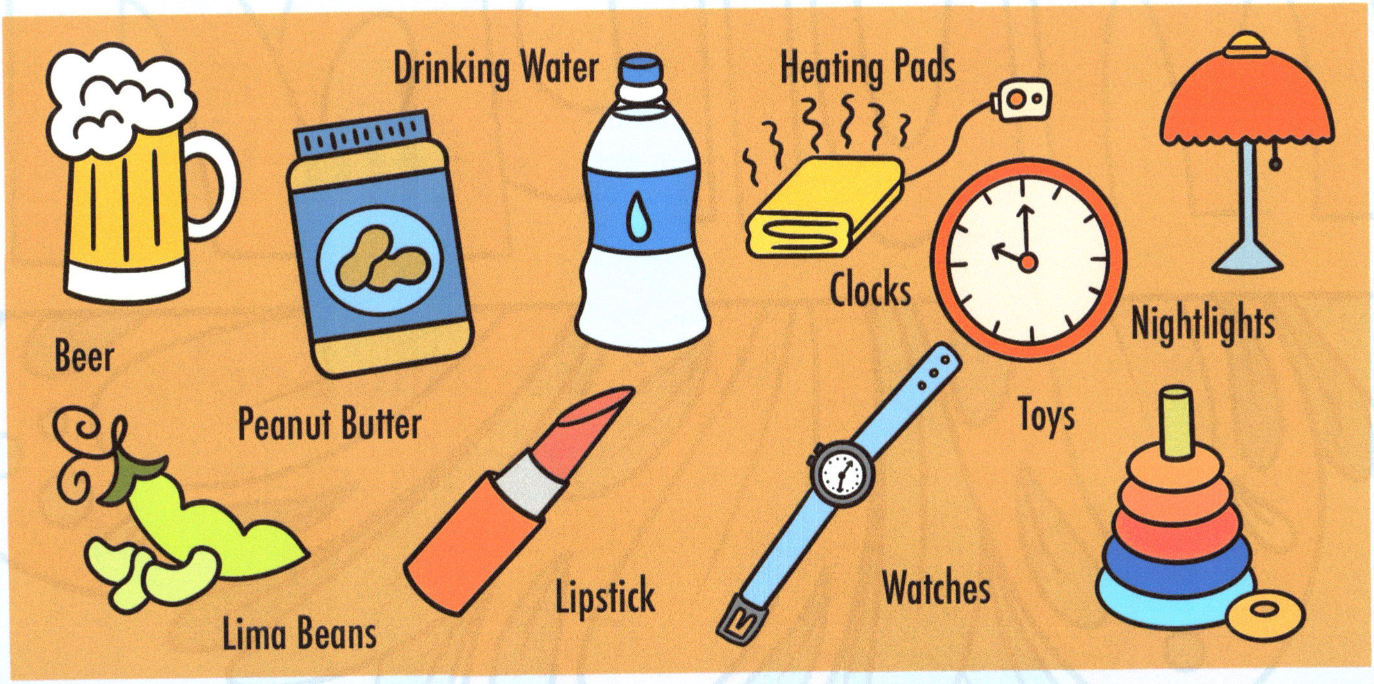
Beer
Peanut Butter
Drinking Water
Heating Pads
Clocks
Nightlights
Lima Beans
Lipstick
Watches
Toys

Ra
Be
Ba
Sr
The End!
remember to:
Believe
Dream
Achieve
Ra
Sr
Ba
Ca
Sr
More Bearific® books
on bearific.com

Katelyn Lonas

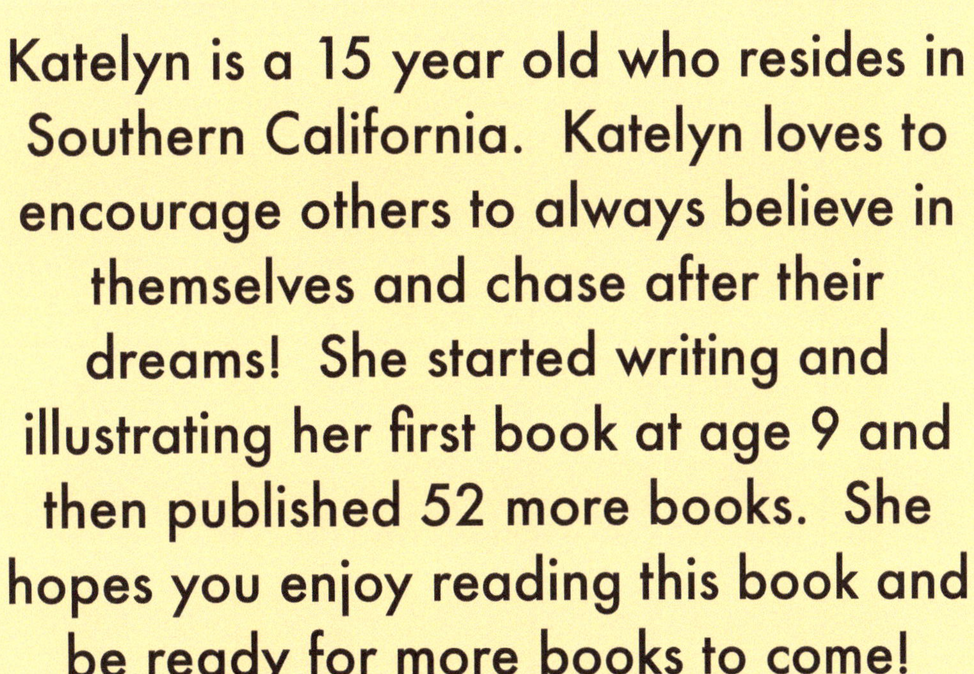

Katelyn is a 15 year old who resides in Southern California. Katelyn loves to encourage others to always believe in themselves and chase after their dreams! She started writing and illustrating her first book at age 9 and then published 52 more books. She hopes you enjoy reading this book and be ready for more books to come!

dium .025	Strontium 84.468	Barium 137.328	Radium 226.025	Strontium 84.468	Bari 137.3
20 Ca lcium .078	4 Be Beryllium 9.012	12 Mg Magnesium 24.305	20 Ca Calcium 40.078	4 Be Beryllium 9.012	12 M Magne 24.3
38 a dium .025	38 Sr Strontium 84.468	56 Ba Barium 137.328	88 Ra Radium 226.025	38 Sr Strontium 84.468	56 B Bari 137.3
20 Ca lcium .078	4 Be Beryllium 9.012	12 Mg Magnesium 24.305	20 Ca Calcium 40.078	4 Be Beryllium 9.012	12 M Magne 24.3
38 a dium .025	38 Sr Strontium 84.468	56 Ba Barium 137.328	88 Ra Radium 226.025	38 Sr Strontium 84.468	56 B Bari 137.3
20	4	12	20	4	12

www.ingramcontent.com/pod-product-compliance
Ingram Content Group UK Ltd.
Pitfield, Milton Keynes, MK11 3LW, UK
UKHW060113300726
14090UKWH00002B/163

* 9 7 8 1 9 5 5 0 1 3 2 4 6 *